THE HYMNS OF CHARLES WESLEY

A STUDY OF THEIR STRUCTURE

THE HYMNS OF CHARLES WESLEY

A STUDY OF THEIR STRUCTURE

by
R. NEWTON FLEW
M.A., D.D.

WIPF & STOCK · Eugene, Oregon

Wipf and Stock Publishers
199 W 8th Ave, Suite 3
Eugene, OR 97401

The Hymns of Charles Wesley
A Study of Their Structure
By Flew, R. Newton
Copyright©1953 Methodist Publishing - Epworth Press
ISBN 13: 978-1-4982-0497-2
Publication date 9/15/2014
Previously published by Epworth Press, 1953

Every effort has been made to trace the current copyright
owner of this publication but without success. If you have any
information or interest in the copyright, please contact the publishers.

TO

MY DEAR BROTHER AND SISTER

EDWIN HOWARD FLEW

AND

ROSALIE STRONG

Didst Thou not make us one,
 That we might one remain,
Together travel on,
 And bear each other's pain,
Till all Thy utmost goodness prove,
And rise renewed in perfect love?
  (*M.H.B.*, *716*)

ABBREVIATIONS USED

M.H.B.   *Methodist Hymn-book* of 1933.

L.B.   'Large Book' of 1780. In this Lecture always cited in the 1782 edition, from the facsimile edition.

P.W.   *Poetical Works of John & Charles Wesley*, 13 vols.

CONTENTS

	FOREWORD	9
	INTRODUCTION: THE ORDERLY STRUCTURE OF CHARLES WESLEY'S HYMNS	15
	Come, Holy Ghost, our hearts inspire. *What shall I do my God to Love.*	
1.	THE HYMNS OF JOHN WESLEY	26
	Father of all, whose powerful voice. *Peace, doubting heart! my God's I am.*	
2.	THE OCCASIONAL HYMNS OF CHARLES WESLEY	32
	HYMN FOR THE KINGSWOOD COLLIERS *Glory to God, whose Sovereign grace*	
	HYMN BEFORE PREACHING AT PORTLAND *Come, O Thou all victorious Lord*	
3.	THE HYMNS ON THE LORD'S SUPPER	42
	Son of God, triumphant rise. *Father, Son, and Holy Ghost.*	
4.	HYMNS ON VARIOUS DOCTRINES	48
	THE UNIVERSAL FATHERHOOD OF GOD *Father, whose everlasting love*	
	PERFECT LOVE *Love divine, all loves excelling*	
	THE DOCTRINE OF ASSURANCE *How can a Sinner know*	
5.	VERSIONS AND PARAPHRASES OF SELECT PSALMS	60
	My heart is full of Christ, and longs	

CONTENTS

6. SHORT HYMNS ON SELECTED PASSAGES OF THE HOLY SCRIPTURES — 66

    THAT HAPPIEST PLACE
    Thou Shepherd of Israel, and mine

    THE AARONIC BLESSING
    Come, Father, Son, and Holy Ghost

    THE CHRISTIAN VERSION OF THE JEWISH CREED
    When quiet in my house I sit

INDEX — 80

FOREWORD

THE ORIGINAL source of this Lecture is traceable to the Methodist habit of taking the *Hymn-book* into the secret place, where the soul prepares for the business of the day and 'freely talks with God'.

Those Methodists who observe and treasure this part of our tradition know why we say to Christians of other communions that our *Hymn-book* is our liturgy, both in public worship and in private prayer. We know that this book is 'a little body of experimental and practical divinity', and we admire the method of teaching theology through these hymns. Dr Henry Bett opened our eyes to the literary value, the sense of wonder, the authentic note of passion, which mark the 'Large Book' of 1780. It was a Cambridge historian of genius, one who spoke from outside our tradition, who first praised it in terms which none of us would ever have dared to use, but which we knew were true for us. Bernard Manning's words are now familiar to those who love the Hymns of Charles Wesley, but they cannot be repeated too often for the sake of others. Writing of the 1780 book, he said: 'You may think my language about the hymns extravagant: therefore I repeat it in stronger terms. This little book ranks in Christian literature with the Psalms, the *Book of Common Prayer*, the Canon of the Mass. In its own way it is perfect, unapproachable, elemental in its perfection. You cannot alter it except to mar it; it is a work of supreme devotional art by a religious genius.'

When Bernard Manning said these words for the first time, I was present. He was reluctant to publish the essay when some of us asked for it, and we were only successful later, when John Telford's request was joined to our entreaties. That was the beginning of a new day in the study of Wesley's Hymns. No Methodist who can learn from the printed word ought to be without *The Hymns of Methodism*, by Dr Bett; *The Hymns of Wesley and of Watts*, by Manning.

He cannot afford to be without the two books of Dr J. Ernest Rattenbury, written out of a masterly survey of the original sources and with unfailing sympathy and insight. All these books are devout and alive. But there are other debts to be acknowledged.

This present study has been written with one question uppermost in the mind, suggested by an essay[1] by Canon Charles Smyth, the Rector of St Margaret's, Westminster, to whom I offer grateful thanks for permission to give prominence to this quotation: 'As Prebendary Wilson Carlile of the Church Army used to say: "You cannot expect a converted old boozer to get much out of Choral Matins". In this connexion it is worth remembering that the one book which did strike home to the converted old boozer of the eighteenth century was *A Collection of Hymns for the Use of the People called Methodists*, and that its compiler was not afraid of Systematic Biblical theology.'

This hint was surely enough to send any Methodist back to the book of 1780. Day by day the hymns were re-read. The leading question now had become: 'Would this hymn have been understood by a converted boozer?' The answer, almost invariably, was: 'Yes! Certainly; if the boozer was really converted.'

This *Collection of Hymns* is slowly being recognized for what it really is: a liturgical miracle. But miracles provoke the mind, and stir it to seek to explain. Some explanations are offered in the following pages, the chief being a suggestion that we should seek our clue in the structure of thought, in the very pattern of the hymn, as it was in the mind of Charles Wesley, before he put pen

[1] *The Genius of the Church of England* (S.P.C.K., 1947), p. 40.

to paper. I have noticed that very often he makes his meaning clear by first announcing the theme, and the 'divisions' by which he is proposing to expound it. This is the way of a good teacher, and the open secret of a lucid preacher. Charles Wesley is not ashamed to have 'divisions', and to announce them at the beginning. With such a mind you know where you are.

A preliminary illustration may be given here, from the hymn which James Montgomery mentions with especial praise, and which has found its way into many hymn-books: 'Christ, whose glory fills the skies.' This is called in the original book of 1740: 'A Morning Hymn.' The theme is announced in the first verse. Christ is the true, the only light. Charles Wesley is leaning on the opening verses of St John's Gospel: 'The life was the light of men', 'That was the true light.' Before the first verse closes he has told us in his prayer, what we are going to pray for.

Dayspring from on high, be near;
Daystar, in my heart appear.

The prayer to Christ as the Dayspring from on high (Lk 1_{78}) is expounded in the second verse. The prayer to the Daystar to appear 'in my heart' (2 P 1_{19}) is the subject of the third verse: 'Visit then this soul of mine.' Bernard Manning comments somewhere on the Pauline habit of invoking the gigantic machinery of the Incarnation to smash a tiny nut of difficulty or discord, whether at Corinth or Philippi (1 Co 8_9, Phil 2_{1-11}). Charles Wesley has caught that Pauline habit. He takes hold of the Johannine (and Lukan) texts which are the prelude to the Gospel delineation of Christ, and invokes the Light of the world to help 'converted old boozers' to say a reverent and grateful 'Good Morning' to God.

But there is a deeper reason for emphasis on the deliberate intention of the Wesleys to teach, through these hymns, the converted 'boozers', the murderers, the harlots, and the thieves,

This intention they found in the Synoptic Gospels. In Section II in this lecture[2] I have illustrated the purpose of the mission of the Wesleys, from the book of Professor C. H. Dodd, *History and the Gospel*. He points out how deeply embedded in the various strata of the Gospel tradition, is one characteristic habit of our Lord. Jesus is vividly distinguished from other religious personalities of His age, by His consorting with the outcasts of society. He is ever seeking them out, winning them back, passionate in His desire to redeem. This consciousness of mission to the outcasts led Jesus to the Cross. Charles Wesley seems to have comprehended this passion, and to have caught it from the very beginning of his Christian life. Even at Oxford, when he was the first of the Holy Club to be called a 'Methodist', he was visiting the prisoners. Years later, in London, though full of misgivings about death-bed repentances, he is praying for 'the poor malefactors while passing to execution'.[3]

This is only five days after the Whitsunday when he was conscious that the Spirit of God strove with him, and 'by degrees chased away the darkness of my unbelief'. The sense of mission grows stronger. The *Journal* for 11th to 19th July paints a self-portrait. But self is lost in this picture, in all its unconscious loveliness. Here is the devoted classical scholar-poet talking to the condemned felons in Newgate. He is especially attentive to the 'poor black that had robbed his master'. On the day of execution there is amid the narrative a terse five words: 'I got upon the cart.' Here is the evangelist loving the children he had begotten in the Gospel, to the very end, and riding with them in the cart from Newgate to Tyburn. The picture is completed by the story of their execution. It was indeed a strange hanging. The condemned expressed

[2] Page 36, *infra*.   [3] *Journal of Charles Wesley*, I.96 (26th May 1738).

some concern, 'how we should get back to our coach', and behaved as men 'going to meet their Lord, ready for the Bridegroom'.

This picture reveals Charles as already equipped by God with the sympathy which could read the hearts of condemned felons, and the readiness to talk to them with words they could understand. In this he is very like His Lord. There are revealing entries in the *Journal* such as this: 'I went . . . to Newgate; shamefully unwilling' (5th October 1738). 'I went to Newgate with my usual reluctance' (10th March 1739). But both these entries are prefaces to stories of astonishing victories. Victories are only won at a cost.

If the following pages, with their attempt to enter into the purpose, the doctrine, and the structure of the hymns of such a man, could induce twelve Methodists to begin and continue the habit of meditating on one of the great hymns of Charles Wesley every day, I should have my reward. But if the analysis of the hymns they study does not convince them that there is a 'normal pattern', I must beg them to remember that to recover the original pattern they will often have to refer to the thirteen volumes of the *Poetical Works of John and Charles Wesley*. Alas, these volumes are rare. But I think it is true to say that Charles Wesley has an orderly mind beyond all others of the great hymn-writers. One doesn't perceive it at first. But when the hymn is studied, the order is there. In the Church of St Mary at Hitchin, there is an 'Angel Screen' to which men come from afar to admire. At first the screen seems beautiful, and delicately wrought, but confused and intricate. Is there a key to the meaning? Yes, if you look at one place—the upper part of the carvings. There are angels with intertwined wings, and each angel has one of the material things which were used at the Crucifixion. There is the wooden cross, the crown of thorns, the spear which pierced His side, the nails, the hammer, the scourge, the sponge, and the seamless robe. At last you see the design of this work of art. Each one of those material things is held by an angel, as it were in adoration, and they are bearing to heaven these emblems of the world's redemption, in wonder and praise.

As I have considered hymn after hymn by Charles Wesley for many years now (I began the habit as a boy away from home at school) I have often been puzzled at first, but now I see more clearly their meaning. Meditation has a way of ending in adoration; and all the time you are not alone, even in the secret place with the door shut. You find yourself murmuring:

> *Ah! show me that happiest place,*
> *The place of Thy people's abode,*
> *Where saints in an ecstasy gaze,*
> *And hang on a crucified God;*
> *Thy love for a sinner declare,*
> *The passion and death on the tree;*
> *My spirit to Calvary bear,*
> *To suffer and triumph with Thee.*

INTRODUCTION

THE ORDERLY STRUCTURE OF CHARLES WESLEY'S HYMNS

IN THE Methodist Church there are many folk who know quite a number of hymns, as we say, by heart. This is not the result of effort, deliberate and enforced, like the learning and repeating of selections from *Paradise Lost*, or the *Golden Treasury*, in the days when we were young. No, the hymns just become part of our mental furniture because we have sung them so many times, said them almost as often, in private converse with our Lord.

To one in our communion, whose mastery of our *Hymn-book* is almost unequalled, I put these questions not long ago: 'Would you say that hymns of Charles Wesley lodge more easily in the memory than the great translated hymns of John? Or than most (save the very greatest) of Isaac Watts? Or even than the majestic medieval hymns, whether in the original Latin or in their English dress?' The answer was, to each question: 'Yes'. And he added with his usual humility: 'I don't know why it is so. But I'd like to know.'

Our Cambridge neighbour, Bernard Manning, whose vivid mind danced through our *Hymn-book*, shedding fresh gleams on forgotten treasures, and shaming us by our neglect of our inheritance, throws one ray of light on the question:

'Let us notice, first, a simple but useful virtue which Wesley practises in almost every hymn. I mean, that he binds his verses, not merely by rhyme, not merely by comparative thought, but by verbal references which, without our noticing them, lead us from line to line.

Wesley gives us no jumps in language to distract us from what he and we are saying. I choose a verse at random:

> *Thou waitest to be gracious still;*
> *Thou dost with sinners bear,*

the second *Thou* carries us on from the first;

> *That, saved, we may Thy goodness feel,*

we of this third line is *sinners* of line 2,

> *And all Thy grace declare.*

Thy grace is a repetition of the idea in *Thy goodness* of line 3.

'It is the technique that the careful reader notes in Macaulay: every sentence is linked with the preceding sentence by a word or an allusion.'

Without doubt, our poet is helping our infirmity by this stylistic habit. But, greatly daring, I would roam for a time in the comparatively untrodden field of the thought-structure of particular hymns. How does the thought develop as the hymn proceeds? Is there a discernible reason why verse three of any hymn should be in that particular position? Or could it exchange places with verse two or verse four?

There are eight hymns by F. W. Faber in the present *Hymn-book*, and of course their place is due to their popularity. Bernard Manning calls him 'wishy-washy,' but allows that 'O come and mourn with me awhile' (*M.H.B.*, 187), 'Saviour bless us ere we go' (*M.H.B.*, 692), 'Was there ever kindest Shepherd' (*M.H.B.*, 318), show us Faber at his best. There are traces of orderly arrangement in the first two. But compare this last hymn with any of the three Shepherd hymns of Wesley, which cannot be counted among Wesley's best: 'Happy soul that, free from harms, Rests within his Shepherd's arms' (No. 13 in 1782; 390 in 1904; *P.W.*, V.293); 'Jesus, great Shepherd

of the sheep' (487 in 1782; 693 in 1904; *P.W.*, V.32–4);
'Jesus the good Shepherd is; Jesus died the sheep to save'
(554 in 1876; 394 in 1904; 621 in 1933; *P.W.*, VIII.46).
Faber and Charles Wesley shared a common devotion
to our Lord. Neither of them is ashamed to let his heart
speak. Both of them understood that the word Shepherd,
in its biblical usage, carries the message of redemption
through the Cross. Yet there is no movement of thought
in Faber's hymn (318). Verse 6,

> *For the love of God is broader*
> *Than the measures of man's mind,*
> *And the heart of the Eternal*
> *Is most wonderfully kind,*

could be promoted to verse two, or to verse three, or to
verse four, with hardly any perceptible violence to the
structure of the hymn. The fifth verse with its yearning
for more simple love, and its saccharine ending, is almost
palpably untrue. Its attempt at paradox,

> *There is joy for all the members*
> *In the sorrows of the Head,*

gives an impression which Faber could not have foreseen.
This is joy with penitence left out; love equated with
kindness. Faber is pointing forward to Ella Wheeler
Wilcox.

Contrast 'Jesus the good Shepherd is'. The hymn is a
clear-cut, orderly exposition of the Twenty-third Psalm,
with the Johannine interpretation of the Good Shepherd
guiding the thought throughout. There is no redemption,
in the New Testament sense of the word, unless there are
foes in whose presence the pilgrim can feast unafraid, and
a valley of the shadow of death through which he can be
guided by his divine Companion. Charles Wesley traces
back to its source in Christ this deliverance from fear,
this light amid the very shadow of death. He ends, as so

often, with the 'strong finish', the life in eternity, while poor Faber ends with a bewildered wistful wonder: 'O if only.'

The main thesis, which I submit with diffidence to those with greater knowledge of hymnology than I possess, is that Charles Wesley's hymns can be analysed; that they have a coherent and intelligible structure of thought, and that this habit of orderly composition is due to his desire to teach Christian doctrine to ordinary people. Their counterpart in prose would be orderly sermons with the divisions clearly marked, as contrasted with sermons destitute of divisions.

Some examples will now be given of varieties of this design or pattern, discernible in many hymns, and showing divisions which could be used by preachers who cared to expound the hymn. The first example is the magnificent hymn to the Holy Spirit imploring His aid in interpreting the Bible.

HYMN 305

M.H.B. (1933)

85 in *L.B.* (1782), 87 (1830 and 1876), 256 (1904), and *P.W.*, I.238–9; written about 1739–40.

The original title was preserved until 1904: '*Before reading the Scriptures*'

>   1. *Come, Holy Ghost, our hearts inspire,*
>   *Let us Thine influence prove,*
>   *Source of the old prophetic fire,*
>   *Fountain of light and love.*
>
>   2. *Come, Holy Ghost, for moved by Thee*
>   *The prophets wrote and spoke;*
>   *Unlock the truth, Thyself the key,*
>   *Unseal the sacred Book.*

3. *Expand Thy wings, celestial Dove,*
   Brood o'er our nature's night;
   On our disordered spirits move,
   And let there now be light.

4. *God, through Himself, we then shall know,*
   If Thou within us shine,
   And sound, with all Thy saints below,
   The depths of love divine.

It is not surprising that there are traces of uncertainty in the various editions of the *Hymn-book* as to the original reading in verse 1, line 4. Did Charles Wesley write 'fountain of light' or 'fountain of life'? Dr George Osborn preferred 'life'. In 1782 and in an edition of 1798, the word 'life' is printed. In the editions from 1830 onward, the word 'light' is always found. If Charles Wesley did write 'fountain of life' instead of the more daring 'fountain of light', subsequent editors have improved on the master's work. See below for the biblical connexion of the concepts, 'light' and 'life'.

The theme or text is contained in the last two lines of the first verse: 'Source of the old prophetic fire, Fountain of light and love'. The three divisions are (1) the Holy Spirit as Source of the prophetic fire; (2) the Holy Spirit as the Fountain of Light; (3) the Holy Spirit as the Fountain of divine Love.

(1) *Source of prophetic fire*

The second verse contains the statement of the first function of the Holy Spirit; He is the Spirit of truth (J 14_{17}), bearing witness to Christ (J 15_{26}), and guiding into all the truth (J 16_{13}). He is the key; He can unseal the sacred Book.

(2) *Fountain of Light*

The third verse begins with a daring imaginative flight, back to the creation of the world: *The Spirit was brooding upon the face of the waters. And God said, Let there be light: and there was light* (Gn 1_{2-3}, R.V. marg.)

Then the thought returns to the New Creation, which is now proceeding in our disordered spirits. There is a clear reference here to Ps 36_{8b-9}, where the loving-kindness of God is portrayed under the concepts of life and light, as two parallel descriptions.

> Thou shalt make them drink of the river of thy pleasures.
> For with thee is the fountain of life:
> In thy light shall we see light.

The same parallel is found in other passages:

> That I may walk before God in the light of life.
> (Ps 56_{13}, R.V. marg.)

> Lo, all these things doth God work . . .
> To bring back his soul from the pit,
> That he may be enlightened with the light of life.
> (Job 33_{29-30}, R.V. marg.)

By his delicate reminiscences of biblical passages such as these, Charles Wesley has provided us with doctrinal riches in four lines, not unworthy of comparison with any verse of that more famous—but more loosely-built—medieval hymn, the *Veni Creator Spiritus* itself.

(3) *Fountain of Love*

The reminiscence of Psalm 36_9 is continued. *In thy light shall we see light*—'God, through Himself, we then shall know', and we shall 'sound the depths of love divine'. But there is inserted a characteristic note of Methodist spirituality, *with all Thy saints below*. The crowd of witnesses in the visible Church, delighting in the fellowship which only the Spirit can give, is never far away from the thought and song of Charles Wesley. You could say with utter truth that Charles Wesley is constantly rejoicing to be one of a mob! But it is a Christian mob; it is 'the church of pardoned sinners, exulting in their Saviour'.

HYMN 77

M.H.B. (1933)

First published in 1749. 207 (1782), 216 (1830, 1876), 66 (two verses omitted, 1904); *P.W.*, IV.446.

The original poem from which the following eight verses are taken was headed: *After a Recovery*. John Wesley inserted it in the Section: *For Believers Rejoicing*.

1. *What shall I do my God to love,*
    My loving God to praise?
    The length, and breadth, and height to prove,
    And depth of sovereign grace?

2. *Thy sovereign grace to all extends,*
    Immense and unconfined;
    From age to age it never ends;
    It reaches all mankind.

3. *Throughout the world its breadth is known,*
    Wide as infinity;
    So wide it never passed by one,
    Or it had passed by me.

4. *My trespass was grown up to heaven;*
    But far above the skies,
    In Christ abundantly forgiven,
    I see Thy mercies rise.

5. *The depth of all-redeeming love*
    What angel tongue can tell?
    O may I to the utmost prove
    The gift unspeakable.

6. *Deeper than hell, it plucked me thence;*
    Deeper than inbred sin,
    Jesus's love my heart shall cleanse
    When Jesus enters in.

7. *Come quickly, gracious Lord, and take*
   Possession of Thine own;
   My longing heart vouchsafe to make
   Thine everlasting throne.

8. *Assert Thy claim, maintain Thy right,*
   Come quickly from above;
   And sink me to perfection's height,
   The depth of humble love.

This outburst of adoration is the sequel to ten verses of penitent confession of wandering from God, and of repeated lapses into sin. Praise such as this can only be understood in the light of forgiveness such as Christ bestows. To the rest of mankind it seems too intense, too passionate, even meaningless. But if Charles Wesley errs here, in his extravagance of praise, he errs in good company. He builds this song on the words of the prayer in Ephesians (3_{17-18}): 'That you, being rooted and grounded in love, may have power to comprehend with all the saints what is the breadth and length, and height and depth, and to know the love of Christ which surpasses knowledge.' Charles Wesley alters Paul's order by interchanging 'breadth' and 'length' and announces his text and divisions in the first verse:

The length, and breadth, and height to prove,
And depth of sovereign grace.

(1) *The 'length'*. This is interpreted in a temporal sense.[1] From age to age God's sovereign grace has a meaning for all men, not for a chosen few, nor only in one period.

(2) *The Breadth* (verse 3). This is interpreted spatially; God has not left any place unvisited by His perpetual Presence. Charles Wesley introduces the note of humility and penitence even here:

[1] The modern reader may be referred to Oscar Cullmann's book, *Christ and Time* (1951), pp. 37-54, for the early Christian conception of time as a straight line, not a circle.

So wide it never passed by one,
Or it had passed by me.

We shall surely agree with Dr Rattenbury[2] that this one couplet contains the real argument against the pitiless 'decrees' as taught in eighteenth-century Calvinism. His ultimate appeal is to facts, and the conviction that Charles Wesley and his readers know God to be One with a love which surpasses knowledge is a fact which can be verified.

(3) *The Height* (verse 4). So far these terms have been interpreted by a traditional method used by a long line of expositors, who saw an allusion to the fourfold structure of the Cross. The length and breadth were supposed to signify the Apostolic Commission to go into all the world, and preach the Gospel; the humanity of our Lord was the depth, and His Divinity the height. But at this point, Charles Wesley throws overboard the fancies of the expositors, and steers his own course. 'My trespass was grown up to heaven', and yet His mercies rise higher yet. He would have echoed the great Scot[3] who deemed it impiety, even blasphemy, to measure his own sins, his many sins, against the mercies of God as shown us in Christ.

(4) *The Depth* (verse 5). It would be difficult to see how Charles Wesley interpreted the depth, if we were shut up to the six verses which the 1933 book has meted out to us, with niggardly hand. We are left with a half-shrouded suspicion that Charles Wesley has nothing more to say, and is using a method familiar to him of referring the explanation to the angels. Fortunately we can cite here what the committee left out:

Deeper than hell, it plucked me thence;
Deeper than inbred sin,
Jesus's love my heart shall cleanse
When Jesus enters in.

[2] *Evangelical Doctrines of Charles Wesley's Hymns*, p. 88.   [3] Robert Bruce.

This is indeed no milk for babes, which is all that we should have if we were left to the angels alone. This is indeed the strong meat which Charles Wesley hardly ever fails to give us when he is approaching his finale. This is surely the 'knock-out blow', dear to the heart of Bernard Manning, and to others also, including St Paul! But no, not quite the finish which Charles Wesley is making for: there is a final verse which is necessary to describe what Charles Wesley and St Paul mean by the words 'height' and 'depth'. After verse 6 in the modern book this verse should be re-inserted.

> *Assert Thy claim, maintain Thy right,*
> *Come quickly from above;*
> *And sink me to perfection's height,*
> *The depth of humble love.*

We are left with the paradox which is familiar to the saints. The height of perfection is also the depth of humble love. Charles Wesley may be indebted to Bengel's *Gnomon* (1742) for the sobriety of his exegesis of Ephesians 3_{18}, and for his use of the traditional meanings attached to 'length' and 'breadth'. But his verses on height and depth are his own expositions, and they ring true. St Paul is speaking . . . of the magnitude of that which it will take them all their strength to apprehend—the Divine mercy, especially as now manifested in the inclusion of the Gentiles, the Divine secret, the Divine purpose for mankind in Christ'.[4] Charles Wesley would have surely rebelled against the comment of one other learned modern interpreter, who, in referring us for the explanation of length, breadth, depth, height, in Ephesians, to the measurements of the heavenly Jerusalem in Revelation 21_{16}, says: 'The heavenly inheritance is conceived as a Cube!'

Recent studies have emphasized the varieties of metre

[4] Armitage Robinson.

used by Charles Wesley; his skilled and incessant use of
the art of allusion, and the art of repetition; his 'supreme
cunning'[5] in the choice of words by which he can intro-
duce into the Watch-Night hymn, composed mainly in
simple Anglo-Saxon words, the two epithets, 'fugitive' and
'millennial'; and his use of the chiasmus, of which he was
an accomplished master. It is not to be thought of that
such an artist would confine himself to one plan or pattern
in building up the thought of his hymns. Perhaps the
following classification, which I have found of help in my
study of the Wesley hymns in the main *Hymn-books* and
the *Poetical Works*, may serve as guidance for others who
study the hymns in private, and use them for the nourish-
ment of the life of devotion:

(1) The Hymns of John Wesley.
(2) Occasional Hymns.
(3) The Hymns on the Lord's Supper.
(4) Hymns on Various Doctrines.
(5) Versions and Paraphrases of Select Psalms.
(6) Short Hymns on Selected Passages of the Holy
    Scriptures.

[5] Bernard Manning.

ONE

THE HYMNS OF JOHN WESLEY

THESE HYMNS only concern my present subject because of the contrast in structure which they present to hymns of Charles Wesley. Amid the debate which long has been proceeding as to the hymns which should be credited to John Wesley, there seems to be one certainty; John is the author of the paraphrase on the Lord's Prayer, 'Father of all! whose powerful voice'. The full hymn is printed in all editions from 1780 to 1904. This is all that is left in *M.H.B.* (1933)

HYMN 47

1. *Father of all! whose powerful voice*
    Called forth this universal frame;
   Whose mercies over all rejoice,
    Through endless ages still the same:

2. *Thou by Thy word upholdest all;*
    Thy bounteous love to all is showed,
   Thou hear'st Thy every creature's call,
    And fillest every mouth with good.

3. *Giver and Lord of Life, whose power*
    And guardian care for all are free,
   To Thee, in fierce temptation's hour,
    From sin and Satan let us flee.

4. *Thine, Lord, we are, and ours Thou art;*
    In us be all Thy goodness showed.
   Renew, enlarge, and fill our heart
    With peace, and joy, and heaven, and God.

5. *Father, 'tis Thine each day to yield*
Thy children's wants a fresh supply;
Thou cloth'st the lilies of the field,
And hearest the young ravens cry.

6. *On Thee we cast our care; we live*
Through Thee, who know'st our every need:
O feed us with Thy grace, and give
Our souls this day the living bread.
                                              Amen.

This can be compared for its content and structure with several hymns of Charles on the same theme, and especially with a hymn of ten verses with eight lines to each verse, among the *Hymns on the Four Gospels*, in *Poetical Works*, XI.200–2 (about 1762).

In this hymn of Charles you know exactly where you are, in every verse. The first verse is devoted to 'Our Father which art in heaven, Hallowed be Thy name'. The next verse begins, 'Thy Kingdom come'. But Charles is well aware that the Kingdom of God is the theme of the teaching of Jesus, and must have a lengthier exposition. So two verses expound 'the first dominion', and two verses the second appearing of our Lord. The sixth verse begins: 'Give us this day our daily bread.' Incidentally, it may be noted that Charles interprets our daily bread as celestial manna, as 'the imperishable meat'. The other verses (7–10) are all carefully in order, each verse devoted to a single clause of the Lord's Prayer.

The honouring of the order and thought of the original words of our Lord is carefully carried through in two other hymns by Charles Wesley in different metres (*Poetical Works*, X.178–9, 179–84).

The second of these contains twenty verses, including the hymn 'From trials unexempted' in four verses, which has appeared in the 1876 *Hymn-book*, and has maintained its position in the subsequent revisions. These two hymns were left in MS.

Contrast any of these with the majestic nine long verses which John Wesley divided into three parts as an exposition of the Lord's Prayer. The first part (225 in 1782, 235 in 1830 and 1876, 42 in 1904, 47 in 1933), is designed as a paraphrase of 'Our Father which art in heaven; Hallowed be thy name'. But apart from the word 'Father', in the first line, and the phrase 'In heaven thou reignest' at the beginning of the second verse, John uses none of the words of our Lord. He gives no other hint that he is expounding the Lord's Prayer. The reader, if given the choice between the Lord's Prayer and Apostle's Creed, might justifiably guess that he was reading an Addisonian version of the Creed. It is easy to understand why the revisers in 1933 decided, in loyalty, to retain three verses out of the nine, and rearranged the verses in almost complete disregard of its original purpose, so that the cry for deliverance from temptation comes before the petition for daily bread.

The contrast between John's early verse and the mature, carefully revised, verses of Charles is not really fair, but it does serve to illustrate the difference between hymns made by the method of elaborate paraphrasing, and hymns made by the method of faithful submission to the order and language of the Scriptures. It may be likened to the difference between the rococo period of architecture, with its elaborate ornamentation, its scrolls and arabesques and cherubim, and the austerity of the classical revival. Charles owed more to his classical studies than his knowledge of Greek poetry. There is a sweet, homely simplicity about their structure that reminds us of the Greeks. At any moment amid the mass of lesser verse, his genius may take wings.

We now turn to a great hymn, which is usually attributed to John Wesley.

HYMN 500
M.H.B. (1933)
264 (1782); 272 (1830 and 1876); 467 (1904)

1. *Peace, doubting heart! my God's I am:*
    Who formed me man, forbids my fear;
   The Lord hath called me by my name;
    The Lord protects, for ever near;
   His blood for me did once atone,
   And still he loves and guards His own.

2. *When, passing through the watery deep,*
    I ask in faith His promised aid,
   The waves an awful distance keep,
    And shrink from my devoted head;
   Fearless their violence I dare;
   They cannot harm, for God is there.

3. *To Him mine eye of faith I turn,*
    And through the fire pursue my way;
   The fire forgets its power to burn,
    The lambent flames around me play;
   I own His power, accept the sign,
   And shout to prove the Saviour's mine.

4. *Still nigh me, O my Saviour, stand!*
    And guard in fierce temptation's hour;
   Hide in the hollow of Thy hand,
    Show forth in me Thy saving power,
   Still be Thy arms my sure defence,
   Nor earth nor hell shall pluck me thence.

5. *When darkness intercepts the skies*
    And sorrow's waves around me roll,
   When high the storms of passion rise,
    And half o'erwhelm my sinking soul;
   My soul a sudden calm shall feel,
   And hear a whisper: Peace; be still!

If the hymn 'Peace, doubting heart! my God's I am' is by John Wesley, as Dr Bett[1] has given us reason to believe, John has proved that he could write a very great hymn. It is founded upon the text of Isaiah 43_{1-3}. This accounts for the double metaphor of water and fire which governs the structure of the hymn.

But now thus saith the Lord that created thee, O Jacob, and he that formed thee, O Israel, Fear not: for I have redeemed thee, I have called thee by thy name; thou art mine.
When thou passest through the waters, I will be with thee; and through the rivers; they shall not overflow thee; when thou walkest through the fire, thou shalt not be burned; neither shall the flame kindle upon thee.
For I am the Lord thy God, the Holy One of Israel, thy Saviour: I gave Egypt for thy ransom, Ethiopia and Seba for thee.

In the original hymn of seven verses, John Wesley has faithfully adhered to the order of this passage for three verses. Then the next verse shows that he has remembered Isaiah 40_{12}: 'Who hath measured the waters in the hollow of his hand?'

He appeals to God: Still nigh me, O my Saviour stand!, and then the original hymn (verse 5) continues the metaphor of 'the watery deep' by using the story of Peter walking on the water.

> *Since Thou hast bid me come to Thee*
>   *(Good as Thou art, and strong to save)*
> *I'll walk o'er life's tempestuous sea,*
>   *Upbourne by the unyielding wave,*
> *Dauntless, though rocks of pride be near,*
> *And yawning whirlpools of despair.*

This verse was omitted in 1933. The last verse of the

---

[1] *The Hymns of Methodism* (3rd Edn., 1945), 29–35. But I have doubts! Did John shout (verse 3)? Charles loves the word, and may have induced John to put it in.

original hymn returns to the metaphor of the fire: 'Though in affliction's furnace tried.'

The conclusion of this analysis is, that, if this hymn was his work, John at his best is not so careful about the structure as Charles is at his best.

But we can be grateful to John at his best, when he translates the Spanish hymn by an unknown author: 'O God, my God, my all Thou art' (425 in 1782, 437 in 1830 and 1876, 429 in 1904, 471 in 1933. Verse 6 omitted in last two revisions).

Here John Wesley's structure was subjected to two controls; the first the control of Ps 63, of which this is a poetical version; and the second the control of the unknown Spaniard. The result is a structure following faithfully the order of the original psalm, and a hymn worthy of the commendation given to it by a noted Anglican hymnologist:[2] 'One of the most melodious and perfect hymns we possess for public worship.' We may note that, in this instance, John seems indisposed to follow Charles in Christianizing the psalm. There is no mention of Jesus Christ or His work.

[2] E. H. Bickersteth, Bishop of Exeter.

TWO

THE OCCASIONAL HYMNS OF CHARLES WESLEY

THIS TITLE includes a multitude of hymns, but I should like to use it for hymns written by Charles Wesley out of his personal experience of the working of God with His people. The first clear example is on 23rd May 1738, 'a hymn upon my conversion'. But he says that he was 'persuaded to break off for fear of pride. Mr Bray coming, encouraged me to proceed in spite of Satan. I prayed Christ to stand by me, and finished the hymn.' It was 'Where shall my wondering soul begin'.

Dr Thomas Jackson attributes to this early period the verses, 'Congratulations to a Friend upon believing in Christ', and thinks that the friend was his brother John. But though we are left in uncertainty about most of the particular 'occasions' on which the hymns were composed, we can infer from the titles that the hymns had their firm seat in life (*Sitz im Leben*, as the expressive German phrase puts it), their sure anchorage in God's grace, God's saving activity, in the lives of human beings. Each one of them was part of the gift of the Spirit entrusted to this particular servant of Christ, Charles Wesley.

The next clear example is: *On the conversion of a common Harlot*. He tells her story with delicacy and restraint in his *Journal* under the dates 15th–20th Feb. 1739. But before this he had faithfully followed in the steps of His Lord, whose mission was specially to the outcasts. Less than two months after his conversion, he was visiting at Newgate the 'poor black that had robbed his master', and who was sentenced to death. He was teaching him and other 'malefactors', his father's hymn: 'Behold the

THE HYMNS OF CHARLES WESLEY 33

Saviour of mankind.' He was singing with them the words of Dr Watts, when they were awaiting death in the cart at Tyburn.

> *A guilty, weak, and helpless worm,*
> *Into Thy hands I fall:*
> *Be thou my strength and righteousness,*
> *My Saviour, and my all.*

'We prayed Him in earnest faith to receive their spirits. I could do nothing but rejoice. . . . We left them going to meet their Lord.'[1]

Among these 'Occasional' hymns, prompted by the experience of itinerant evangelism, two may be selected as examples of careful, artistic structure: the hymn written for the Kingswood Colliers, composed in 1739 or 1740, and the hymn written on the Isle of Portland, in the midst of his visit in 1746.

HYMN FOR THE KINGSWOOD COLLIERS

No. 195 (1782); 203 (1830 and 1876); 366 (1904). John Telford gravely comments: 'The last two, which belonged to drunken colliers, are wisely omitted from such a collection as this'. The reference is to the 1904 edition.

1. *Glory to God, whose sovereign grace*
    Hath animated senseless stones;
    Called us to stand before His face,
    And raised us into Abraham's sons!

2. *The people that in darkness lay,*
    In sin and error's deadly shade,
    Have seen a glorious gospel day,
    In Jesu's lovely face displayed.

[1] *Journal of Charles Wesley,* 19th July 1738.

3. *Thou only, Lord, the work hast done,*
　　And bared thine arm in all our sight;
　Hast made the reprobates thine own,
　　And claimed the outcasts as thy right.

4. *Thy single arm, almighty Lord,*
　　To us the great salvation brought,
　Thy Word, Thy all-creating Word,
　　That spake at first the world from nought.

5. *For this the saints lift up their voice,*
　　And ceaseless praise to Thee is given;
　For this the hosts above rejoice,
　　We raise the happiness of heaven.

6. *For this, no longer sons of night,*
　　To Thee our thankful hearts we give;
　To Thee, who call'dst us into light,
　　To Thee we die, to Thee we live.

7. *Suffice that for the season past*
　　Hell's horrid language filled our tongues,
　We all Thy words behind us cast,
　　And lewdly sang the drunkard's songs.

8. *But, O the power of grace divine!*
　　In hymns we now our voices raise,
　Loudly in strange hosannas join,
　　And blasphemies are turned to praise!

The theme is stated in the first two verses. 'We, the converted colliers of Kingswood, are become, like Zacchaeus, Sons of Abraham (Lk $19_{9\text{-}10}$). We now understand what Jesus meant when He said that if His disciples held their peace, the stones will cry out (Lk 19_{40}). We know we were as senseless as stones. But, now, we stand before the face of God. We know what the prophet meant when he said (Is 9_2): "The people that walked in darkness have seen a great light." This has now come true in us.' The title-text might well be: *Light after Darkness*. The divisions of thought are clearly marked:

(1) *This is the Lord's doing* (verses 3 and 4).
(2) *Our answer is gratitude, and complete dedication* (verses 5 and 6).
(3) *The proof of the power of grace divine is our changed lives* (verses 7 and 8).

(1) *This is the Lord's doing*
This is the first natural confession of the men who know that they were once in darkness, and now are light in the Lord (Eph 5_8): 'This is of God; I could never have changed myself.' But, natural as it seems, it is supernatural also. It is due to a divine revelation, and is a fulfilment of a divine purpose, long ago declared, by prophets and Psalmist:

'The Lord hath made bare his holy arm, in the eyes of all the nations; and all the ends of the earth shall see the salvation of our God' (Is 52_{10}.)

> 'And he shall set up an ensign for the nations,
> And shall assemble the outcasts of Israel.'
> (Is 11_{12}.)

'Mine house shall be called an house of prayer for all peoples.
'The Lord God which gathereth the outcasts of Israel saith, Yet will I gather others unto him, beside his own that are gathered' (Is 56_{7-8}.)[2]

> 'He gathereth together the outcasts of Israel.
> He healeth the broken in heart.'
> (Ps 147_{2-3}.)

[2] It is surely not without significance that this verse, referring to the gathering of the outcasts, immediately follows the verse quoted by our Lord when He justified His cleansing of the temple. The authorities would argue: 'This Revolutionary has already distinguished himself by his declared mission to the outcasts. He proposes perhaps to admit the Gentiles to his company. What next?'

Charles Wesley's thought in verse 3 is thus linked with the very few passages of the Old Testament which contain the word 'outcasts'. This care for the outcasts of society is selected by Professor C. H. Dodd with unerring insight, as the characteristic which distinguished Jesus as an historical personality from the other religious personalities of His time, and which is attested by a great variety of 'forms' and in the Gospel tradition. Parables, aphorisms, poetical sayings, dialogues, stories of various kinds, taken from all the four main strata of the Synoptic Gospels (Mark, Q, Matthew's special source, and Luke's special source)—all bear witness to the passion of our Lord to redeem the outcasts. It is not surprising that a hymn-writer so saturated in the Scriptures, and especially in the Gospels, should have early grasped this dominant motive, linked it with the Old Testament promises, and discerned in this redeeming work the baring of the arm of the Almighty, the great salvation (verse 4, line 2), the mighty power of the Word in a new creation. Yet all this he read into the changed lives of the colliers at Kingswood, and into 'the conversion of a common harlot'.[3]

(2) *Our response is gratitude and complete dedication* (verses 5 and 6)

There is a reference (verse 5, line 3) to the joy in the presence of the angels of God over the 'one sinner that repenteth' (Lk 15_{10}). We share their praise, their thanks. 'To Thee our thankful hearts we give.' As in the Communion Service, 'this our sacrifice of praise and thanksgiving' is identical with our offering and our presenting ourselves unto God as a 'reasonable, holy, and living sacrifice'. This is one act, both gratitude and dedication. Both are due to the consciousness that the Christian, in

---

[3] See *P.W.*, I.93–4; *Journal of Charles Wesley* for 15th–20th February 1939; cf. the description of the work at Kingswood by Mr Joseph Williams of Kidderminster, quoted in Thomas Jackson, *Life of Charles Wesley* (1841), pp. 195–7.

life and in death, belongs to the Lord (Ro 14$_8$). 'What is thy only comfort in life and in death?' is the first question of the noble Heidelberg Catechism. And the answer, unsurpassed for depth, peace, simplicity, and beauty, strikes the authentic note of the Christian life: 'That I, with body and soul, both in life and in death, am not my own, but belong to my faithful Saviour Jesus Christ, who with His precious blood has fully atoned for all my sins.' In this answer the learned young Calvinist scholars of Heidelberg and the Kingswood Methodist colliers can join hands. This firm conviction of belonging to Christ, of being Christ's men, not our own, unworthy though we are, is essential to Christian holiness.

(3) *The proof of the power of grace divine is our changed lives*
Of course verses 7 and 8 had to be omitted. They sound so crude and amusing in the ears of respectable modern congregations. Perhaps some swearing is due to bravado or poverty of vocabulary. But is it easy to control the tongue? Is there no foul, licentious language from which men need to be saved? And why are there so few of those who need saving from their poverty of vocabulary, or from their own unclean talk, turning to praise with us in our churches?

HYMN WRITTEN BEFORE PREACHING AT PORTLAND

The other notable hymn composed to meet a particular occasion in his evangelistic ministry has been preserved in its entirety in all the standard hymn books from the death of the Wesleys to the present day. We are fortunate to possess an account of Charles Wesley's visit to the Island of Portland from his own pen:

June 4th, 1746.... It rained incessantly and blew a hurricane. ... By nine at night we were glad to reach W. Nelson's house in Portland.

June 6th. . . . I preached to a house-full of staring, loving people. Some wept, but most looked quite unawakened. At noon and night I preached on a hill in the midst of the island. Most of the inhabitants came to hear; but few, as yet, feel the burden of sin, or the want of a Saviour.

June 8th. . . . After evening service we had all the islanders that were able to come. I asked, 'Is it nothing to you, all ye that pass by?' About half-a-dozen answered, 'It is nothing to us', by turning their backs; but the rest hearkened with greater signs of emotion than I had before observed. I found faith at this time that our labour would not be in vain.

June 9th. . . . At Southwell, the fartherest village, I expounded the song of Simeon. Some very old men attended. I distributed a few books among them; rode round the island; and returned by noon, to preach on the hill; and by night, at my lodgings. Now the power and blessing came. My mouth and their hearts were opened. The rocks were broken in pieces, and melted into tears on every side. I continued exhorting them, from seven till ten, to save themselves from this untoward generation. We could hardly part. I left the little society of twenty members confirmed and comforted.

The following hymn, 'written before preaching at Portland', as Charles Wesley expressly tells us, was probably composed in the four days, 5th–8th June:

HYMN 347
M.H.B. (1933)
84 (1830, 1876); 305 (1904); *P.W.*, V.124

1. *Come, O thou all-victorious Lord,*
   Thy power to us make known;
   Strike with the hammer of Thy word,
   And break these hearts of stone.

2. *O that we all might now begin*
   Our foolishness to mourn,
   And turn at once from every sin,
   And to our Saviour turn!

3. *Give us ourselves and Thee to know,*
    In this our gracious day;
    Repentance unto life bestow,
    And take our sins away.

4. *Conclude us first in unbelief,*
    And freely then release;
    Fill every soul with sacred grief,
    And then with sacred peace.

5. *Impoverish, Lord, and then relieve,*
    And then enrich the poor;
    The knowledge of our sickness give,
    The knowledge of our cure.

6. *That blessèd sense of guilt impart,*
    And then remove the load;
    Trouble, and wash the troubled heart
    In the atoning blood.

7. *Our desperate state through sin declare,*
    And speak our sins forgiven;
    By perfect holiness prepare,
    And take us up to heaven.

When Charles Wesley presents us with a hymn of seven verses of four lines each, we may expect that he will entrust us with his theme in the first verse, and then explain his subject in three sections of two verses each. Here he follows that normal practice. He has naturally been fascinated by the sight of the quarrymen working in or near the quarries from which, seventy or eighty years before his visit, Sir Christopher Wren extracted the stone for the building of St Paul's Cathedral. Charles Wesley noticed the rhythmic smiting of 'the hammer'. There is also a direct allusion in the first verse to Jer 23_{29}. 'Is not my word like as a fire, saith the Lord, and like a hammer that breaketh the rock in pieces?'

The three divisions are three prayers: for
  (1) *The Gift of repentance* (verses 2 and 3), and
  (2) *The Blessings which Christ gives* (verses 4 and 5),
  (3) *The Deliverance promised at the Cross* (verses 6 and 7).

(1) *The Gift of repentance*
Few of the inhabitants 'as yet feel the burden of sin or the want of a saviour'. This was the comment in the *Journal* after the first service at Portland. The second verse uses twice the word 'turn' for 'repent'. This is the meaning of the original Hebrew word, 'turn' or 'turn back'. This is the simplest and clearest way of defining repentance: a turning from every sin, a turning to our Saviour; and the meaning is still further developed in the third verse. The gift of repentance results at once in another gift, the recognizing of ourselves and of Christ. This is life (verse 3, line 3) instead of death. This is how Jesus takes our sins away.

(2) *The Blessings which Christ gives*
The gifts which follow are expressed in a series of verbal surprises, which show how penitence is the condition of every blessing. First, we are to be shown our unbelief and only then find release. There is first sacred grief, and then sacred peace. The impoverishment precedes the riches, as the knowledge of our sickness precedes the knowledge of our cure.

In these verses, crammed with paradox, the chief difficulty to modern ears is likely to be the word 'conclude'. It is quoted from Ro 11_{32} (A.V.). The paradox must be credited to St Paul, or rather to the insoluble problem which he is probing. In a passage of rhythmic prose, which reminds us of the parallelism of Hebrew poetry, he cries out his daring prayer of hope:

> *For God hath concluded them all in unbelief,*
> *That he might have mercy upon all.*

CHARLES WESLEY

The difficult word 'conclude' disappears in the modern versions. Its place is taken by the less rhythmical 'shut up all unto disobedience' or the even less poetical word, 'consigned'. The word means 'involve in', 'give over to'; St Paul is declaring that there is a divine purpose behind the fact that all men are in some degree or another 'given over to disobedience' and allowed to sin. It is that God may show His infinite compassion to all.

(3) *The Deliverance promised at the Cross* (verses 6 and 7)

The first two lines of verse 6 take up and define the last two lines of verse 5. 'The knowledge of our sickness' becomes 'that blessèd sense of guilt', or the load that is to be removed. Then for the first time in the hymn, Christ is lifted up on His Cross. This appears only in the petition, 'wash the troubled heart in the atoning blood'. Those who think that all mention of 'cleansing by the blood' is aesthetically improper, or morally revolting, should be referred to one who wrote more majestic prose than any of the moderns. In commenting on the ritual acts of a cultus now for him quite obsolete, the author of the Epistle to the Hebrews contrasts these ceremonial sprinklings with the effect of the voluntary sacrifice of Christ: 'How much more shall the blood of Christ, who through the eternal Spirit offered himself without blemish to God, purify your conscience from dead works to save the living God' (9_{14}). We ought not to censure indiscriminately the references to 'blood' in Charles Wesley's hymns.[4] They are usually bound closely to the Holy Scriptures, and as here are used as imagery of the unique sacrifice of Jesus Christ in redeeming mankind from their sins. Here, in successive lines, the threefold gift is given by the Crucified—pardon and holiness and heaven.

[4] See Dr Rattenbury on this: *Evangelical Doctrines*, 204-7; *Eucharistic Hymns*; 106-18.

THREE

THE HYMNS ON THE LORD'S SUPPER

THESE HYMNS are clearly in a class by themselves. Their arrangement in six sections is due to the doctrinal argument of Dr Brevint, which precedes them in all editions, and on which they are a poetical commentary. 'Charles Wesley gives Brevint wings', says Dr Rattenbury in his invaluable modern treatise.[1] He notes the fidelity with which the Wesleys follow the argument of Brevint. He explains the number of devotional verses, very often of two-versed hymns, that have little connection with the section in which they are placed. These hymns of general consecration would be most suitable in the intervals in any largely-attended Communion Service. The need for them as well as the use of them is clearly shown in the letter, quoted by Dr Rattenbury, from John Fletcher to John Wesley:

As the number of communicants is generally very great, the time spent in receiving is long enough for many to feel their devotion languish for the want of outward fuel. In order to prevent this, you interrupt from time to time, the service of the Table, to put up a short prayer, or to sing a verse or two of a hymn, and I do not doubt but many have found the benefit of that method.

Among the longer hymns there are examples of what I have called the normal pattern or structure—first the announcement of the theme of the whole theme of the hymn, and then the exposition in two or three well defined parts.

Among the Post-Communion Hymns there is one

[1] *The Eucharistic Hymns of John and Charles Wesley*, 1948.

characteristic hymn of Charles Wesley, twice in the first verse bidding us to shout.

HYMN 164 IN 'HYMNS ON THE LORD'S SUPPER'
P.W., I.170

1. *Sons of God, triumphant rise,*
   Shout th' accomplish'd Sacrifice!
   Shout your sins in Christ forgiven,
   Sons of God, and heirs of heaven!

2. *Ye that round our altars throng,*
   Listening angels, join the song:
   Sing with us, ye heavenly powers,
   Pardon, grace, and glory ours!

3. *Love's mysterious work is done!*
   Greet we now th' accepted Son,
   Heal'd and quicken'd by His blood,
   Join'd to Christ, and one with God.

4. *Christ, of all our hopes the seal;*
   Peace Divine in Christ we feel,
   Pardon to our souls applied:
   Dead for all, for me He died!

5. *Sin shall tyrannize no more,*
   Purged its guilt, dissolved its power;
   Jesus makes our hearts His throne,
   There He lives, and reigns alone.

6. *Grace our every thought controls,*
   Heaven is open'd in our souls,
   Everlasting life is won,
   Glory is on earth begun.

7. *Christ in us; in Him we see*
   Fulness of the Deity.
   Beam of the Eternal Beam;
   Life Divine we taste in Him!

> 8. *Him we only taste below;*
> *Mightier joys ordain'd to know,*
> *Him when fully ours we prove,*
> *Ours the heaven of perfect love!*

After his invitation to praise God addressed to forgiven sinners, and his appeal to the listening angels, the theme is announced in a single line—

> *Pardon, grace and glory ours!*

This threefold theme is followed in each pair of the next six verses. The divisions are:

(1) *Pardon* (verses 3 and 4)
(2) *Grace* (verses 5 and 6)
(3) *Glory* (verses 7 and 8)

It is strange that a perfectly constructed hymn, stating the Christian doctrine of grace, has only been given a reluctant entrance (two and a half verses only) into one of our official hymn-books, that of 1830. Note the delicate way in which the theme of Glory is, as it were, bowed in, by the last line of verse 6.

HYMN 574

M.H.B. (1933)

418 (*L.B.*) 430 through the nineteenth century; 562 (1904); *P.W.*, III.333

Let us turn to that great hymn which, as Dr Rattenbury says, in width and depth has never been surpassed as a vow of utter and complete devotion to Christ. It has always been accessible, to the Methodist people, unaltered and unabridged, since the year 1745, when it made its first appearance in the *Sacramental Hymns*.

> 1. *Father, Son, and Holy Ghost,*
>   *One in Three, and Three in One,*
> *As by the celestial host,*
>   *Let Thy will on earth be done;*
> *Praise by all to Thee be given,*
> *Glorious Lord of earth and heaven.*
>
> 2. *Vilest of the sinful race,*
>   *Lo! I answer to Thy call;*
> *Meanest vessel of Thy grace,*
>   *Grace divinely free for all,*
> *Lo! I come to do Thy will,*
> *All Thy counsel to fulfil.*
>
> 3. *If so poor a worm as I*
>   *May to Thy great glory live,*
> *All my actions sanctify,*
>   *All my words and thoughts receive;*
> *Claim me for Thy service, claim*
> *All I have and all I am.*
>
> 4. *Take my soul and body's powers;*
>   *Take my memory, mind, and will,*
> *All my goods, and all my hours,*
>   *All I know, and all I feel,*
> *All I think, or speak, or do;*
> *Take my heart, but make it new.*
>
> 5. *Now, O God, Thine own I am,*
>   *Now I give Thee back Thine own;*
> *Freedom, friends, and health, and fame*
>   *Consecrate to Thee alone:*
> *Thine I live, thrice happy I;*
> *Happier still if Thine I die.*

> 6. *Father, Son, and Holy Ghost,*
>   *One in Three, and Three in One,*
>   *As by the celestial host,*
>   *Let Thy will on earth be done;*
>   *Praise by all to Thee be given,*
>   *Glorious Lord of earth and heaven.*

Charles Wesley indicates, as it were by a signpost the passage in Brevint's Preface, on which he is writing this hymn: *Lo, I come to do Thy will, O God*. It is the text from Psalm 40, which the author of the Epistle to the Hebrews chooses (10_{1-10}) in order to show the contrast between whole burnt offerings and the perfect sacrifice of the death of Christ. 'It is impossible that the blood of bulls and goats should take away sin.' Christ's sacrifice can cleanse the conscience because it is a voluntary act of perfect obedience to the way of God.

But Charles Wesley prepares carefully for the special conception of our sacrifice of ourselves, our souls and bodies. He does not begin his hymn as Brevint begins his paragraph, with the quotation from the psalm. He begins with the Holy Trinity and passes swiftly to the familiar prayer: 'Thy will be done, On earth as it is in heaven.' He knows that he must start from the familiar things, in order to teach the doctrine of the only sacrifice which we can make to God. The call of God to us is to do His perfect will—that is, to offer to Him 'this our sacrifice of praise and thanksgiving'; to 'present unto Him ourselves, our souls and bodies to be a reasonable, holy, and lively sacrifice unto Thee'.

The main theme of the hymn is summarized in the last two lines of verse 2:

> *Lo! I come to do Thy will,*
> *All Thy counsel to fulfil.*

The divisions are:—

(1) *Verse 3. God's claim is absolute.* Therefore I build my large petitions for entire holiness on that claim.

(2) *Verse 4. The response of man must be all or nothing.* Therefore I offer my all; I offer my heart—but it must be created anew.

(3) *Verse 5. Acceptance is certain now.* It is noticeable that the last two lines of verses 2, 3, 4, and 5 contain the movement of thought that is made in this great hymn.

FOUR

HYMNS ON VARIOUS DOCTRINES

To call this section 'Doctrinal Hymns' would be to apply to an unspecified number of hymns a title more appropriate to all of the Hymns of Charles Wesley in the 1780 book. The claim of John has been richly vindicated: 'This book is, in effect, a little body of experimental and practical divinity.' Martineau's tribute to the book, in a letter to Miss Winkworth, can never be repeated too often: 'After the Scriptures, the grandest instrument of popular religious culture that Christendom has ever produced.' But there are many hymns, not included in the other five classes, which do teach a specific doctrine with force and lucidity, and sometimes with extraordinary charm.

THE UNIVERSAL FATHERHOOD OF GOD

First among Christian doctrines is the belief that God is Father. It is the first word in the Lord's Prayer, though the teaching of Jesus has often been strangely obscured in the history of the Church. Dr John Scott Lidgett in his great book on *The Fatherhood of God* has shown how the doctrine was recovered at the time of the Reformation, and lost again. This loss should not be attributed to John Calvin, who considered the supreme test of election to be 'the deeply rooted persuasion of the fatherly love of God', implanted in believers by the Holy Spirit Himself. In spite of Calvin's profound insistence on 'God's immense love towards us so that we can be called the sons of God', this note was by no means clearly sounded in eighteenth century England. There is no treatment of the Fatherhood of God in the Sermons of Bishop Butler.

But in the Methodist teaching, this emphasis was revived. 'The hymns have one presupposition and only one, linking them all together, and eventually manifested by them all—the universal Fatherhood of God' (Lidgett). This explains his search after mankind and His gift to them. The conviction of the fatherly love of God lies behind the passionate assertion of the capacity of all men to be saved, to live in communion with God as children commune with their Father.

Let us take some illustrations.

HYMN 75
M.H.B. (1933)
39 (1830 and 1876); 65 (1904); *P.W.*, III.3

1. *Father, whose everlasting love*
    Thy only Son for sinners gave,
    Whose grace to all did freely move,
    And sent Him down the world to save.

2. *Help us Thy mercy to extol,*
    Immense, unfathomed, unconfined;
    To praise the Lamb who died for all,
    The general Saviour of mankind.

3. *Thy undistinguishing regard*
    Was cast on Adam's fallen race;
    For all Thou hast in Christ prepared
    Sufficient, sovereign, saving grace.

4. *The world He suffered to redeem;*
    For all He hath the atonement made;
    For those that will not come to Him
    The ransom of His life was paid.

5. *Why then, Thou universal Love,*
    Should any of Thy grace despair?
    To all, to all, Thy bowels move,
    But straitened in our own we are.

> 6. *Arise, O God, maintain Thy cause!*
> *The fullness of the Gentiles call;*
> *Lift up the standard of Thy Cross,*
> *And all shall own Thou diedst for all.*

This hymn had originally seventeen verses. It was not included in the Large Book (1780), but soon, after 1791, room was made for it. The omissions (eleven in all) were skilfully made, and the structure of the thought was not only undamaged, but clarified. Seven of the omitted verses give proof texts from the Scriptures, and the other four are examples of the assertion in verse 5, that 'straitened in our own we are'.

The theme is stated in the first two lines: the everlasting love of the Father in giving His only Son for sinners (Jn 3_{16}). The divisions are:

(1) *The meaning of 'grace'* (verse 1, lines 3 and 4, and verse 2, lines 1 and 2).
(2) *Christ died for all* (verse 2, line 3).
(3) *Therefore Christ can save all* (verse 2, line 4).

(1) *The meaning of 'grace'*
Verse 3 takes up the theme as declared in the first verse. 'Grace' is defined as God's loving action in sending Christ to save sinners; grace is given to fulfil the original purpose for Adam's fallen race. The word 'undistinguishing' is a reminiscence of Acts 11_{12}, where Peter says: 'The Spirit bade me go with them making no distinction.'

(2) *Christ died for all* (verse 4)
It was to atone for the sin of the whole world that He died. The texts used to prove this include: 'Behold the Lamb of God, which taketh away the sin of the world' (Jn 1_{29}), 'God so loved the world' (Jn 3_{16}), and 'I if I be

lifted up from the earth will draw all men unto myself' (Jn 12_{32}).

(3) *Therefore Christ can save all*

He is the Universal Saviour of mankind (verse 2, line 4) because God is universal Love (verse 5, line 1). The conclusion is: Therefore none need despair of receiving the grace of God (verse 5, line 2).

The Epilogue (verse 6) is the echo of a psalm (perhaps 74_{22}: 'Arise, O God, plead thine own cause') joined to the yearning hope of St Paul (Ro 11_{25}) for the salvation of all Israel when the 'fulness of the Gentiles' be come in. The phrase means 'the full completed number', 'the Gentile world as a whole'. Charles Wesley surely has in mind the conclusion of this passage: 'that he might have mercy upon all'.

The whole hymn, written at a time of fierce controversy as it was, clearly states a reasoned case. Further, it shows that the doctrine of the Fatherhood of God could not be stated by Charles Wesley except in the light of the doctrine of the Grace of God, as active in Christ. To expect a separate doctrinal hymn on the Fatherhood of God to be wrapped up with other hymns in the first section of a hymn-book, without a declaration of the Sonship of Christ and the redeeming work of Christ, was to Charles Wesley unthinkable.

Surely he is right.

PERFECT LOVE

HYMN 431

M.H.B. (1933)

374 (1782); 426 (1904); *P.W.*, IV.219. First published in *Hymns for Those that seek and Those that have Redemption in the Blood of Jesus Christ* (1747).

1. *Love divine, all loves excelling,*
    Joy of heaven, to earth come down;
  Fix in us Thy humble dwelling,
    All Thy faithful mercies crown:
  Jesu, Thou art all compassion,
    Pure, unbounded love Thou art;
  Visit us with Thy salvation,
    Enter every trembling heart.

2. *Breathe, O breathe Thy loving Spirit*
    Into every troubled breast,
  Let us all in Thee inherit,
    Let us find that second rest:
  Take away our bent to sinning,
    Alpha and Omega be
  End of faith as its Beginning,
    Set our hearts at liberty.

3. *Come, almighty to deliver,*
    Let us all Thy grace receive;
  Suddenly return, and never,
    Never more Thy temples leave:
  Thee we would be always blessing,
    Serve Thee as Thy hosts above,
  Pray, and praise Thee, without ceasing,
    Glory in Thy perfect love.

4. *Finish then Thy new creation,*
    Pure and spotless let us be;
  Let us see Thy great salvation,
    Perfectly restored in Thee;
  Changed from glory into glory,
    Till in heaven we take our place,
  Till we cast our crowns before Thee,
    Lost in wonder, love, and praise.

CHARLES WESLEY 53

The first verse states the theme of the entire hymn. It is a prayer for the indwelling of Christ, who is identified with pure, unbounded love. The metre and opening lines are reminiscent of a poem intended for earthlier ears. The *Song of Venus* in Dryden's *King Arthur* begins:

> Fairest Isle, all isles excelling,
>   Seat of pleasures and of loves;
> Venus here will choose her dwelling,
>   And forsake her Cyprian groves.

For Charles Wesley divine Love is incarnate in a Person whose purpose was a full salvation for every man, and for this he prays.

The three divisions of the original prayer are:

(1) *Prayer for the Holy Spirit.*
(2) *Prayer for the Return of our Lord, the Second Coming.*
(3) *Prayer for the finishing of the New Creation, first on earth and finally in Heaven.*

(1) Prayer that Jesus will breathe the Holy Spirit as He breathed on the disciples (Jn 20_{22}). The love of God hath been shed abroad in our hearts by the Holy Spirit which was given unto us (Ro 5_5). Charles Wesley is justified in speaking in one verse of the indwelling Christ, and in another of the indwelling Spirit. He is following St Paul:

You are not in the flesh but in the Spirit if so be that the Spirit of God dwelleth in you (Ro 8_9).
If Christ is in you . . . if the Spirit of Him that raised up Jesus from the dead dwelleth in you . . . his Spirit that dwelleth in you (Ro $8_{10, 11}$).

How did John Wesley justify his omission of this verse? It is through the Holy Spirit that Christ will become all in all to us. It is through the Holy Spirit that He will finish His new creation, that we may be pure and spotless in His presence. The omission may have been due to an objection of John Fletcher against verse 2 line 5. He rightly argued that to 'take away the *power* of sinning' meant the destruction of man's freedom. Later the word was changed to *bent*. But it is strange that John Wesley and others thought that it did not matter whether the explicit reference to the Holy Spirit was retained or not. They did not see that it is the first thing to be said. Love is the fruit of the Holy Spirit. It ought to be stated plainly in a hymn like this that the Holy Presence of God Himself is ever active in His Church in the hearts of His people; that he is working for our freedom from sin, and that the life of a Christian man is due to the active love of God from beginning to end. Once this verse reappears we can discern the familiar progress of thought in Charles Wesley's mind. In this verse he describes the Christian life as an inheritance of all things in Christ; as a second Rest, with its glancing allusion to the Rest which remaineth for the people of God (He 3_{18-19}; 4_{1-11}); and as a taking away of our 'bent to sinning'. Thus the One who is the Author and the End of Faith will set our hearts at liberty.

It is a pleasure to add that the Baptist *Church Hymnal* has preserved this verse in the *Revised Edition* of 1933 (Hymn 317). They have overcome the difficulty by the line: 'Take away the love of sinning'.

(2) *Prayer for the Return of our Lord* (verse 3 in the original; verse 2 since 1830)

In the phrase *Suddenly return* . . . there is a reminiscence of Malachi 3_1: 'Behold I send my messenger, and he shall prepare the way before me; and the Lord, whom ye seek, shall suddenly come to his temple.' Charles Wesley has evidently pondered on the fact that the first part of the prophecy is applied to John the Baptist by Mark and Matthew. He identifies 'the Lord whom ye seek' with Jesus. It is Jesus, according to this Christian interpretation, who shall suddenly return to His temples. It is Jesus who shall visit us with His salvation and enter every trembling heart. The return to the Temple is interpreted as implying, for the people of God on earth, unceasing prayer and unceasing praise. The goal of the Christian life on earth is service, the doing of the will of God as the angels do in heaven. This goal is described in the phrase which is rare[1] in Charles Wesley's hymns, 'perfect love.'

(3) *Prayer for the finishing of the New Creation* (verse 4)

The last verse is a prayer for the final vision of God in heaven. The finishing of the New Creation, according to the promise that we shall all be pure and unblemished before Him in love (Eph 1_4, 5_{27}); the progress from glory to glory (2 Co 3_{18}), as we are transformed into the image of our Lord; the casting of our crowns before His throne in heaven (Rev $4_{4,10}$); these provide the picture-language for the description of that which is ultimately indescribable, the bliss of the saints when time is no more. But this hymn with its music and passion is witness to the New Testament conviction that the great salvation perfectly restored in heaven preserves an essential continuity with the salvation already wrought by Christ upon the earth. To this salvation multitudes of the saints have set their seal, testifying that He is true.

The poem of Dryden is read by hundreds; the hymn of Charles Wesley is sung and read by tens of thousands.

[1] J. E. Rattenbury, *Evangelical Doctrines*, p. 280.

THE DOCTRINE OF ASSURANCE

HYMN 377
M.H.B. (1933)

93 (1782); 359 (1904); *P.W.*, V.363

1. *How can a sinner know*
    His sins on earth forgiven?
   How can my gracious Saviour show
    My name inscribed in heaven?
   What we have felt and seen,
    With confidence we tell;
   And publish to the sons of men
    The signs infallible.

2. *We who in Christ believe*
    That He for us hath died,
   We all His unknown peace receive,
    And feel His blood applied;
   Exults our rising soul,
    Disburdened of her load,
   And swells unutterably full
    Of glory and of God.

3. *His love, surpassing far*
    The love of all beneath,
   We find within our hearts, and dare
    The pointless darts of death:
   Stronger than death and hell
    The mystic power we prove;
   And conquerors of the world, we dwell
    In heaven, who dwell in love.

4. *We by His Spirit prove*
   And know the things of God,
   The things which freely of His love
   He hath on us bestowed;
   His Spirit to us He gave,
   And dwells in us, we know;
   The witness in ourselves we have,
   And all its fruits we show.

5. *The meek and lowly heart*
   That in our Saviour was,
   To us His Spirit doth impart,
   And signs us with His Cross:
   Our nature's turned, our mind
   Transformed in all its powers;
   And both the witnesses are joined,
   The Spirit of God with ours.

6. *Whate'er our pardoning Lord*
   Commands, we gladly do;
   And guided by His sacred word,
   We all His steps pursue:
   His glory our design,
   We live our God to please;
   And rise with filial fear divine,
   To perfect holiness.

It is difficult to appreciate the elaborate statement of the doctrine of assurance in this hymn, if we know only the abbreviated modern version. The first verse, which is now (in *M.H.B.*, 1933) set out as two verses, is really a unity. The opening quatrain sets the problem. The second four lines declare that the answer is to be found in the Christian awareness of God which comes through faith in Christ. It is what we have felt and seen. Charles Wesley describes the answer as 'the Marks of Faith'

(*P.W.*, V.363), or, as in the hymn itself, the 'knowledge of the things of God' (verse 4).

SUMMARY

(1) Faith brings peace and freedom (verse 2).
(2) Faith works through love (verse 3).
(3) Faith becomes knowledge (verse 4).
(4) Faith involves a transformation of our nature, (verse 5).
(5) Faith issues in obedience (verse 6).

This fivefold analysis is at every point an explanation of the work of the Holy Spirit according to the Scriptures. It is an account of the things which are given to us through God's revelation in Christ.

(1) *Faith brings peace and freedom* (verse 2)
Since faith is a personal trust in Christ Crucified, we find peace with God, a peace unknown before. The encumbering burden of guilt is taken away. At the Cross the prisoner loses his chains, and cannot but leap for joy.

(2) *Faith works through love* (verse 3)
It is love of a power stronger than death or hell. This love we know to be of a range and quality beyond our old familiar earthly affections, though not superseding them or hostile to them.

(3) *Faith becomes knowledge* (verse 4)
Faith in Christ does not depend on mere feeling; it becomes knowledge of the things of God. The knowledge is not acquired through our own insight or industry, but is the free gift of the Holy Spirit, who dwells within.

(4) *Faith involves a transformation of our nature,* (verse 5)
Faith in Christ leads to humility, the meekness, the

lowliness which was in our Saviour Christ. This too is given at the Cross, and is nothing less than a transformation of the mind. It is as though the Spirit of God made the sign of the Cross over us to signify that our nature is now turned towards Him.

(5) *Faith in Christ issues in obedience* (verse 6)

But, it is the obedience not of a hired servant, but of a son. The word 'fear' is used here in the sense of 'reverence': 'Conduct yourselves with reverence throughout the time of your exile' (1 Peter 1_{17}). This isn't the sense implied in 1 John 4_{18} ('Perfect love casteth out fear'). In Hellenistic Greek the word *phobos* has to do duty for two main meanings; 'dread', or 'terror', and 'reverence'. As 'terror', it is the direct opposite of faith. (Mk 5_{36}; Ro 8_{15}). As 'reverence', it can be joined with 'love'. The fear of God and the love of God can be conjoined as a motive for doing the will of God (Dt 10_{12}). In 1 Peter 1_{17} God is called 'Father' as well as 'Judge'. We are meant to be His children, which means to be men in filial communion with God, men after God's own pattern. This is the way, filial fear—that is, reverence and love.

FIVE

VERSIONS AND PARAPHRASES OF SELECT PSALMS

THE STRUCTURE of these versions is dictated by the purpose of Charles Wesley, which he inherited from Dr Isaac Watts, to Christianize the Old Testament book of praise. But Watts is dominated by the method of paraphrasing. This method was inherited by Watts himself from the Calvinist tradition of Church psalmody based upon the Latin psalter. The early translators of the Psalms, both in England and in Scotland, aimed at an almost literal transcription of the Biblical originals. This literalism, as Watts himself pointed out, was an evil, and led to a sub-Christian use of the Psalms: 'I have long been convinced that one great occasion of this evil arises from the matter and words to which we confine all our Songs. Some of 'em are almost opposite to the spirit of the Gospel: many of them are foreign to the state of the New Testament and widely different from the present circumstances of Christians' (*Works*, IV.147).

The Wesleys endorsed the reformation which was inaugurated by Watts. The first proof is in the first hymn-book, published by John Wesley in 1737 at Charlestown in Georgia. The very existence of this *Collection of Psalms and Hymns* was unknown or forgotten until 1878, when a copy was discovered in London. In 1882 it was reprinted. There are seventy-eight hymns, and a large proportion of them were by Isaac Watts.

In his edition of the Psalms (1719), Dr Watts omitted some, introduced evangelical themes into many, and altered the names of Judah and Israel to England and Scotland. In Psalm 147$_2$ he allowed the name Jerusalem to stand, but there is a drastic transformation of verses 12 to 20 into a highly patriotic 'Song for Great Britain'. The last two verses are:

> He sheweth his word unto Jacob:
> His statutes and ordinances unto Israel.
> He hath not dealt so with any nation:
> Neither have the heathen knowledge of his laws.
> Praise ye the Lord.

Watts' version gives a strangely optimistic view of the religious education of the country in 1719:

> But he hath nobler works and ways,
> To call the Britons to his praise.
> To all the isle his laws are shown;
> His gospels through the nation known;
> He hath not thus revealed his word
> To every land. Praise ye the Lord.

Charles Wesley's changes of the Psalms, if less patriotic, are more polished, more faithful to the Scripture language, and more insistent on the 'saving truth'.

'Watts, because he is dominated by the notion of paraphrasing, puts Scripture very often into his own words; it is not always to the advantage of Scripture. Wesley does little paraphrasing. He puts his own notions into Scripture language, and it is always to their advantage.'[1]

Wherever I have been able to test Charles Wesley's version of the Psalms, I have found that his verses strictly follow the order of the verses in the original. The following hymn is perhaps the noblest example of the transfiguration of a psalm into the glory which is Christ.

Psalm 45

1. My heart is inditing a good matter: I speak of the things which I have made touching the king: my tongue is the pen of a ready writer.

[1] Bernard Manning, *Hymns of Wesley and of Watts*, p. 105.

2. Thou art fairer than the children of men: grace is poured into thy lips: therefore God hath blessed thee for ever.

3. Gird thy sword upon thy thigh, O most mighty, with thy glory and thy majesty.

4. And in thy majesty ride prosperously because of truth and meekness and righteousness.

HYMN 270

M.H.B. (1933)

639 (1830); 568 (1876); 210 (1904); *P.W.*, VIII.102.

1. *My heart is full of Christ, and longs*
    Its glorious matter to declare!
   Of Him I make my loftier songs,
    I cannot from His praise forbear;
   My ready tongue makes haste to sing
    The glories of my heavenly King.

2. *Fairer than all the earth-born race,*
    Perfect in comeliness Thou art;
   Replenished are Thy lips with grace,
    And full of love Thy tender heart;
   God ever blest! we bow the knee,
    And own all fullness dwells in Thee.

3. *Gird on Thy thigh the Spirit's sword,*
    And take to Thee Thy power divine;
   Stir up Thy strength, almighty Lord,
    All power and majesty are Thine:
   Assert Thy worship and renown;
    O all-redeeming God, come down!

4. *Come, and maintain Thy righteous cause,*
    And let Thy glorious toil succeed;
   Dispread the victory of Thy Cross,
    Ride on, and prosper in Thy deed;
   Through earth triumphantly ride on,
    And reign in every heart alone.

Dr W. R. Maltby once put the following question: 'What hymn should Evangelist sing on his way to preach on a Sunday morning?' Many candidates were proposed by others to him out of the 1933 book, notably 599, 924, 465, 785, 572, 390. But finally he affirmed the perfect choice to be Hymn 270: 'It is the malady of modern religion, and of much modern preaching, that we cannot forget ourselves and glory in Christ Jesus. We know something about ourselves, and if the theologians have left anything unsaid, the psychologists have supplied the lack. Our sins, our failures, personal and social, our repentances, our efforts, our strivings—these are our preoccupation. . . . There is in the Christian life man's part and God's part: but what we cannot be persuaded of is that man never finds strength for his own part if he is preoccupied with it, but only when his eyes are on God's part, which is all in all.'[2]

If Evangelist meditates on the movement of this hymn he will be preoccupied with 'God's part' throughout his journey, and the Church where he is to preach will be reached too soon. The opening verse of the hymn, as of the psalm, sets forth the theme of praise of Christ, praise of the glories of the heavenly King. Then the theme of 'God's part' is developed in three verses:

(1) *The Fullness of the Grace of Christ.*
(2) *The Sword of the Spirit.*
(3) *The Victory of the Cross.*

(1) *The Fullness of the Grace of Christ*

First comes the word 'Grace' (verse 2, line 3), the redeeming activity of our King'. Evangelist will be allowed to linger perhaps on that word, and to wonder at the transformation wrought in its meaning. The ordinary Greek word (*charis*) for thanks, or gracefulness, is

[2] *Obiter Scripta* (1952), pp. 109–10.

charged with a dynamic meaning in the vocabulary of St Paul. In his letters the dominant use is in the phrase given to us in the Apostolic Benediction—'the grace of our Lord Jesus Christ'. Grace is God's loving action, God's active favour and mercy to men, contrary to their desert. In the third line there is a glinting reference to the people at Nazareth, listening to Jesus, wondering at the words of grace which proceeded out of His mouth. But the grace was not exhausted at Nazareth. It has been continually 'replenished' since, because that 'never-failing' quality is the essence of the love of God. The word 'fullness', in the Pauline sense of the word, as Dr A. S. Peake taught us in his commentary on Colossians long ago, means 'the fullness of the divine redemptive activity'. This is grace, active in Christ for reconciliation. It was God's good pleasure that this fullness should 'reside' in Christ (Col 1_{21}). As Bengel says, 'this indwelling is the very ground of the reconciling work of Christ'.

(2) *The Sword of the Spirit, which is the word of God* (Eph 6_{17})

Psalm 45 (Prayer Book version) translates verse 4 as '*the word* of truth, meekness, and righteousness'. This, instead of the Authorized Version translation, provides the theme for Charles Wesley's treatment of the power of Christ in verse 3. He is thus enabled to interpret the Word as the gospel message, and to interpret the sword in verse 3 as 'the Sword of the Spirit, which is the word of God'. Thus the warfare for truth, meekness, and righteousness is Christ's campaign in the might of the Holy Spirit. The work of the Holy Spirit, as the living personal presence of God Himself, is essential to the preaching and receiving of the Gospel.

(3) *The Victory of the Cross*

Evangelist will notice that the final paradox, the good news of a Saviour victorious on a Cross, is not reached till the end of his meditation. First, his thoughts have been direct to a Person, and the riches of that Person are inexhaustible, if there is any gospel to be preached at all. The fullness is there in Christ, in the eternal purpose of the Father. That reconciling message is always sustained and empowered by the Presence of God Himself. The piercing point of the gospel is the message of the victory of Christ Crucified and Risen, the only hope of mankind. We do not yet see all peoples subjected to Him: but we do see that Jesus, by the love and humility of His entrance, through that lowly door of sacrifice, into the human heart, has the right and the might to rule the world.

SIX

SHORT HYMNS ON SELECTED PASSAGES OF THE HOLY SCRIPTURES

OF THE groups into which I have divided the hymns for the purpose of this Lecture, this is the largest. They first appeared in two volumes in 1762. They fill four and a half volumes out of the thirteen volumes of the *Poetical Works*, and if we add to these the *Versions and Paraphrases of Select Psalms*, they fill five large volumes. These expository hymns have never yet been subjected to the consideration they deserve. In the light of the modern revival of Biblical theology, they would, I believe, win a favourable verdict for their doctrine, their spiritual insight, and the sober method of interpretation which they employ. Dr Rattenbury says:[1] 'With very few exceptions the allegorical interpretations are convincing, and rarely, as in the case of many allegorists, grotesque'.

These volumes speak both of deep reverence for the sacred Scriptures and of unremitting toil. Fortunately, we have first-hand evidence for his invincible perseverance in the revision of the *Hymns on the Four Gospels and the Acts of the Apostles*. At the end of the five quarto volumes of manuscript, he tells us, in his own handwriting, that during a period of twenty-two years he had carefully revised it no less than eight times:

Finished, April 24, 1765.
Δ Θ
The revisal finished, April 24, 1774.
Δ Θ

[1] *Evangelical Doctrines*, p. 93.

Another revisal finished, Jan. 28, 1779.
Δ Θ
A third revisal finished, Feb. 29, 1780.
Δ Θ
A fifth revisal finished, Aug. 6, 1782.
Δ Θ
A sixth finished, Oct. 28, 1784.
Δ Θ
The seventh, if not the last, Jan. 11, 1786
Gloria Tri-uni Deo!
Δ Θ
The last finished, May 11, 1787.
HALLELUJAH!

The final revision was completed less than a year before he died. Inspiration and hard work, work aiming at perfection, improving little by little on the original inspiration, are certainly not incompatible. A modern student of Milton has spoken of the corrections shown on the original draft of Lycidas as showing, to the least critical reader, 'by what a succession of inspirations a work of consummate art is produced'.[2]

For his habits of composition in the last few years of his life, we have the account of a most reliable eye-witness, Henry Moore, the trusted executor and biographer of John Wesley. He says of Charles:

He rode every day (clothed for winter even if in summer) a little horse, grey with age. When he mounted, if a subject struck him, he proceeded to expand and put it in order. He would write a hymn, thus given him, on a card kept for that purpose, with his pencil, in shorthand. Not infrequently he has come to our house in the City-road, and, having left the poney in the *garden* in front, he would enter, crying, out, 'Pen and ink! Pen and ink!'[3] These being supplied, he wrote the hymn he had been composing. When this was done, he would look round on those present, and salute them with much kindness, give out a short hymn, and thus put all in mind of eternity. He was fond of that stanza upon those occasions:

[2] John Bailey, *Milton* (1915), p. 131.   [3] Italics due to Henry Moore!

> 'There all the ship's company meet
>   Who sailed with the Saviour beneath,
> With shouting each other they greet,
>   And triumph o'er trouble and death:
> The voyage of life's at an end,
>   The mortal affliction is past;
> The age that in heaven they spend
>   For ever and ever shall last.'[4]

The most significant sentence for the purpose of this present study is: 'he proceeded to expand and put it in order'. I suggest that after he had chosen the metre, by long-practised habit of composition, he would select naturally one of several patterns, and notably the structure which has here been described as 'normal'. First the theme in one verse, sometimes in two; then the working out of the theme in two or three or more sections. 'Putting it in order' would also include the happy repetition of words, in order that the verses could more easily dwell in the memories of those who sang or heard or read them. Bernard Manning's examples of this device, given above, could be indefinitely multiplied.

Sometimes toil was not necessary. He could accept a momentary inspiration as the gift of God, and have it transcribed on paper. A few days before he died, as his wife wrote in her hymn-book, he repeated the following lines to her, his last bequest:

> *In age and feebleness extreme,*
> *Who shall a helpless worm redeem?*
> *Jesus, my only hope Thou art,*
> *Strength of my failing flesh and heart;*
> *O could I catch one smile from Thee,*
> *And drop into eternity!*

These words are deeply prized among us.[5] His strength was that he kept glowing in the hearts of multitudes the

---
[4] *The Life of the Rev. John Wesley* (1824), II.369.
[5] *M.H.B.* (1933) *Verses*, No. 47.

conviction of eternity. Many, if not most of the hymns end in the thought of heaven. John Fletcher wrote in a letter to him (15th November 1759), which seems an answer to a doubt of Charles: 'I feel that for you which I do not for myself. I am so assured of your salvation, that I ask no other place in heaven, than that I may have at your feet. I doubt even if Paradise would be a Paradise to me, unless it were shared with you.'

The end for which all his toil was directed was the saving of ordinary folk, and particularly the outcasts. We have noted this at the beginning of his evangelistic course. The closing years saw the same fire steadily burning. The last publication that he sent from the press was a tract of twelve pages. It was called *Prayers for Condemned Malefactors*. In a manuscript note to one of those hymns, he says: 'These prayers were answered, Thursday, April 28th, 1785, on nineteen malefactors who all died penitent. Not unto me, O Lord, not unto me!' He spoke of Christ in words which the meanest and lowest could understand.

THAT HAPPIEST PLACE

HYMN 457

M.H.B. (1933)

Not in 1780 or 1782 editions; 245 (1798); 221 (1799); 228 (1830 and 1876); 423 (1904); *P.W.*, IX.362

1. *Thou Shepherd of Israel, and mine,*
    The joy and desire of my heart,
   For closer communion I pine,
    I long to reside where Thou art:
   The pasture I languish to find
    Where all, who their Shepherd obey,
   Are fed, on Thy bosom reclined,
    And screened from the heat of the day.

2. *Ah! show me that happiest place,*
   The place of Thy people's abode,
Where saints in an ecstasy gaze,
   And hang on a crucified God;
Thy love for a sinner declare,
   Thy passion and death on the tree;
My spirit to Calvary bear,
   To suffer and triumph with Thee.

3. *'Tis there, with the Lambs of Thy flock,*
   There only, I covet to rest,
To lie at the foot of the rock,
   Or rise to be hid in Thy breast;
'Tis there I would always abide,
   And never a moment depart,
Concealed in the cleft of Thy side,
   Eternally held in Thy heart.

This hymn is a comment on the Song of Songs 1,7: 'Tell me, O thou whom my soul loveth, where thou feedest thy flock, where thou makest it to rest at noon.' If all the other *Short Hymns on Selected Passages of the Holy Scriptures* were, by some strange apostasy of the mind, finally judged to be false interpretation, there are those among us who would still claim that this hymn is one of the unapproachable lyrics of devotion. 'An unspeakable treasure of the soul', says Dr Rattenbury, 'this hymn is beyond analysis'.[6] Thousands of ordinary people, for whom Christ Crucified was the centre, the power and the wisdom of life, have taken this hymn into the secret place, and lingered on each line, and found themselves lifted into the heavenly places about which they sang. But it has been deemed equally suitable for public worship among the people called Methodists. If the hymn is beyond analysis, I would dare to set down some of the

[6] *Evangelical Doctrines*, p. 184.

reasons why I join with Dr Rattenbury in regarding this hymn as one of the greatest ever written. If its realities are to be expressed by 'the mystic method', it may be of some moment to point out the distinguishing convictions which set this hymn in a class apart from and above the utterances of classical Mystics.

(*a*) The first and outstanding merit is that Charles Wesley in this lyric never goes beyond New Testament spirituality, as we might have feared in an exposition of a text from the Song of Songs. Dr Clement Webb has pointed out that the mystic writers are distinguished by their use of metaphors of union. It is easy to provide examples: 'being one with God', 'lost in God', or even (as in the *Mirror of Simple Souls* and in Gerlac Peterson) 'glued together as one and the self-same thing.'[7] The use of this language does not at all imply that all mystics habitually teach that the soul of man becomes God; such a confusion is expressly disclaimed by one of the very greatest of them, John Ruysbroeck. But the habitual use of metaphors of union opens the door to a confusion between the creature and the Creator. The devotion of the New Testament is expressed with metaphors of communion, not union. Sometimes Charles Wesley himself forsakes the Scriptural high road. Witness the following:

> *Let all I am in Thee be lost,*
> *Let all I am be God.*
> P.W., I.372 (*in the Hymn on Hebrews* 4_9,
> '*Lord I believe a rest remains*').

> *Make my soul Thy pure abode,*
> *Filled with all the deity,*
> *Swallowed up and lost in God.*
> P.W., II.68 (cf. P.W., III.144, 166).

Contrast such misleading language with the exquisite

[7] E. Underhill, *Mysticism*, pp. 510–12.

precision of this hymn. The first verse speaks of closer communion, and of shelter from the heat of the day. This means exactly what Jesus said and practised.

> Thou, when thou prayest, go into thy room and shut the door,
> And pray to thy Father who is in secret;
> And your Father who sees in secret will reward thee
> (Mt 6:6).

> Come away by yourselves to a lonely place, and rest a while (Mk 6:31).

> And in the morning, a great while before day, he rose and went out to a lonely place, and there he prayed. (Mk 1:35).

There must be a set time for solitariness, or if not for solitariness, for some shelter from the thronging duties and demands of everyday life, from 'the heat of the day'.

(b) Charles Wesley will not contemplate any rest or bliss which cannot be shared. Christ is Charles Wesley's Shepherd because Christ is the Shepherd of the New Israel. This thought constantly saves him from mere individualism. He will find the pasture where all who obey their Shepherd are feeding.

This is indeed the translation into exquisite poetry of the conviction of the Wesleys: 'The Gospel of Christ knows of no religion but social; no holiness, but social holiness.'[8] Contrast this with the utterance of the great theologian of the Middle Ages, Thomas Aquinas, in one of the less happy articles of his *Summa*: 'If there were but one soul alone to enjoy God, it would be blessed, even though it were without a single fellow-creature whom it could love.' But in this article St Thomas separates what God has joined, love of God and love of the neighbour. God's interest in the world is direct, detailed; it is part of His supreme greatness that He cares for every sparrow

[8] *P.W.*, I.xxii.

that falls to the ground. Baron von Hügel instances the Book of Revelation, which 'shows the deepest emotion when picturing all the souls, from countless tribes and nations standing before the throne—an emotion which can, surely, not be taken as foreign to those souls themselves'.[9]

Charles Wesley shares that emotion. He sees clearly that the life and message of Jesus would become meaningless, and the Church of God would lose its deepest roots, if the ultimate destiny of mankind is not a perfected society, in communion with God and with one another through the sharing of the love of God. In this lyric, God is portrayed as revealing His own deepest nature as 'the Good Shepherd, the lover of each single sheep and of the flock as a whole'.[10]

(c) The third positive quality, which characterizes this hymn as supremely true to New Testament religion, is that the centre and object of the devotion is Christ Crucified. The saints are all dependent on a Crucified Man, Whom they all recognize as divine. There is no desire to escape from history. The gospel of pardon and the possibility of holiness alike depend on the Cross. But perhaps the truest and most searching touch in the hymn is in the couplet:

> *My spirit to Calvary bear,*
> *To suffer and triumph with Thee.*

'To suffer'—this is the urgent, day-to-day death to self; this is to regard all the inevitable losses, disappointments, pains and disabilities, as opportunities to be accepted as richly ministrant to our spiritual growth; the words 'to suffer' before the words 'and triumph' signify that God has 'planted the Cross at the heart and centre of the prayer-life'.[11] But the note of renunciation, though unmistakably

[9] *Mystical Element in Religion*, II.254. [10] Ibid, p. 255.
[11] See A. L. Lilley, *Prayer in Christian Theology*, p. 8.

sounded, is not allowed to subdue the triumphant march of this melody. The love which Christ has towards us looks to final victory. Charles Wesley knows that the resting-place of the flock at noon is also the abiding-place for all eternity, and he makes us share his longing for a place in the heart of God.

THE AARONIC BLESSING

HYMN 378

(1933; last four verses only); 252 (1830; 1876); 354 (1904); *P.W.*, IX.65

1. *Come, Father, Son, and Holy Ghost,*
    One God in Persons Three,
   Bring back the heavenly blessing, lost
    By all mankind and me.

2. *Thy favour, and Thy nature too,*
    To me, to all restore;
   Forgive, and after God renew,
    And keep us evermore.

3. *Eternal Sun of Righteousness,*
    Display Thy beams divine,
   And cause the glories of Thy face,
    Upon my heart to shine.

4. *Light in Thy light O may I see,*
    Thy grace and mercy prove,
   Revived and cheered and blessed by Thee,
    The God of pardoning love.

5. *Lift up Thy countenance serene,*
    And let Thy happy child,
   Behold, without a cloud between,
    The Godhead reconciled.

6. *That all-comprising peace bestow*
On me, through grace forgiven;
The joys of holiness below,
And then the joys of heaven.

The Lord bless thee, and keep thee:
The Lord make his face shine upon thee, and be gracious unto thee:
The Lord lift up his countenance upon thee, and give thee peace.

The structure reflects the purpose of Charles Wesley to Christianize the Old Testament. The hymn is a Christian exposition of the Aaronic blessing (Nu 6_{24-6}).

(1) The first two verses are an exposition of 'The Lord bless you and keep you'. This includes the blessings of forgiveness, the renewal of our mind according to the image of Him who created us (Col 3_{10}), and God's sustaining power. The insertion of the words, 'after God renew', shows Charles Wesley's fidelity not only to St Paul's, but also to Luther's teaching. Luther in 1535 defined justification as 'in very truth a regeneration leading to a new life'.

(2) The second two verses expound the words: 'The Lord make his face to shine upon you and be gracious unto you.'

(3) The fifth and sixth verses expound the final sentence: 'The Lord lift up His countenance upon you, and give you peace.' The lifting up of the countenance of God is happily translated into the New Testament image of the privilege of sonship, which is the gift bestowed upon us when we are reconciled to God. The phrase 'That all-comprising peace' is another mark of the mastery of the meaning of words which characterizes Charles Wesley. In the Old Testament, as in the New, peace is not a mere absence of hostilities, it is the inclusive term for all the benefits of God, all the joys of holiness below, and then the joys of Heaven.

It will be noticed that the teaching value of this hymn has been impaired by the omission of the first two verses from our modern *Hymn-book*. It would be difficult for any reader, who has only the last four verses before his eyes, to discover the connexion of these verses with the Aaronic blessing. Did the Committee know that they were amputating the head from the body of a superb benediction?

Only when we understand that this is a hymn addressed to the Blessed Trinity, reinterpreting one of the sublimest prayers of the Old Testament in the light of the New Testament doctrine of the Fatherhood of God, is it possible to enter into and appropriate its value, both for the life of private devotion, and in the theological teaching of the Church.

THE CHRISTIAN VERSION OF THE JEWISH CREED

HYMN 310
M.H.B. (1933)

264 (1904); 328 (1780); *P.W.*, IX.94

Only in the 1876 book are we pointed to the Scripture text (Dt 6_7) which explains the structure of this hymn. The preceding verses (Dt 6_{4-6}) contain the essential creed and duty of Israel, the first text of the Bible which Jewish children have learned to say and to read, 'the confession of faith among all members of the brotherhood of Judaism':[12]

Hear, O Israel: the Lord our God is one Lord: and thou shalt love the Lord thy God with all thine heart, and with all thy soul, and with all thy might. And these words which I command thee this day, shall be upon thine heart: and thou shalt teach them diligently unto thy children, and shalt talk of them when thou sittest in thine house, and when thou

[12] C. G. Montefiore, *The Bible for Home Reading*, I.127.

walkest by the way, and when thou liest down, and when thou risest up.

The last four sentences are expounded consecutively, but by a Christian interpreter, in the four verses of the hymn.

1. 'Thou shalt talk of them when thou sittest in thine house':

> *When quiet in my house I sit,*
>   *Thy Book be my companion still,*
> *My joy Thy sayings to repeat,*
>   *Talk o'er the records of Thy will,*
> *And search the oracles divine,*
> *Till every heartfelt word be mine.*

2. 'And when thou walkest by the way':

> *O may the gracious words divine*
>   *Subject of all my converse be!*
> *So will the Lord His follower join,*
>   *And walk and talk Himself with me;*
> *So shall my heart His presence prove,*
> *And burn with everlasting love.*

3. 'And when thou liest down':

> *Oft as I lay me down to rest,*
>   *O may the reconciling word*
> *Sweetly compose my weary breast!*
>   *While, on the bosom of my Lord,*
> *I sink in blissful dreams away,*
> *And visions of eternal day.*

4. 'And when thou risest up':

> *Rising to sing my Saviour's praise,*
>   *Thee may I publish all day long;*
> *And let Thy precious word of grace*
>   *Flow from my heart, and fill my tongue;*
> *Fill all my life with purest love,*
> *And join me to the Church above.*

(1) In the first verse, the Jewish confession of faith in the unity and uniqueness of God, has been transformed. 'These words' become 'Thy Book', the whole Bible, with the New Testament as well as the Old.

(2) In the second verse the transformation has been completed by the delightful introduction of the story of the walk to Emmaus (Lk 24_{13-35}): 'Was not our heart burning within us, while he spake to us in the way, while he opened to us the scriptures?'

The study of the Book leads to knowledge of the real Presence of Christ with His own. He is the source of everlasting love. 'The reconciling word' of verse 3 is the same as 'the gracious words' of verse 2; both mean 'the Gospel': God with us, companying with us now as Jesus walked and talked with his followers, both in his earthly, and in His Risen Life.

(3) The third verse is Charles Wesley's brave solution of a difficult problem. He has committed himself to following the four divisions of his text. But obviously the act of going off to sleep offers less scope than the other phrases in the text. He does not take refuge, like some modern divines, in the R.V. margin of the Psalmist's word (Ps 127_2), 'So he giveth to his beloved *in* sleep', and detail examples of mysteries elucidated by dreams. But though he is probably not thinking of Psalm 127 at all, he is true to the thought of the psalm. 'Well doth God appoint sleep'. God's good gift of sleep should not be abridged by anxious care for the morrow. It is a parallel to Matthew 6_{28-32}: 'Consider the lilies. . . . Be not therefore anxious', The opposite to the blissful dreams of sleep is the demon form of black care, and the boding fears filling the hours of sleeplessness. There is a reconciling word for believing people; there is the promise of rest of soul, from the lips of Christ. There is a Christian way of going to bed, and its ground is the faithfulness of our Lord, and His reconciling word. We really need not lie awake fearing to-morrow.

G. K. Chesterton speaks of people who are puzzled by 'Consider the lilies', when spoken by Christ, yet who would not be surprised to find that St Francis of Assisi had said: 'I beseech you little brothers, that you be as wise as Brother Daisy and Brother Dandelion; for never do they lie awake thinking of to-morrow, yet they have gold crowns like Charlemagne in all his glory.'[13]

(4) The fourth verse is the quintessence of Christian missionary endeavour distilled into six lines. This is the prayer of Charles Wesley, the evangelist. Evangelism is a duty we are apt to shun. But all the followers of Christ are called to proclaim Christ. Charles Wesley by this verse calls his fellow Christians, when they rise in the morning, to 'publish Christ' throughout the day. One of the greatest of all his hymns is headed: 'For a lay preacher', but Methodists have rightly interpreted the hymn as one to be sung by all who own their unfathomable debt to Christ. It is the hymn[14] which ends with the verse:

> *Enlarge, inflame, and fill my heart*
> *With boundless charity divine!*
> *So shall I all my strength exert,*
> *And love with a zeal like Thine;*
> *And lead them to Thy open side,*
> *The sheep for their Shepherd died.*

[13] *St Francis of Assisi*, p. 137. I owe this reference to Mr Peter J. Collingwood.
[14] *M.H.B.*, 390.

INDEX

AARONIC BLESSING, 74-6
Aquinas, St Thomas, 72

BAILEY, JOHN, 67
Baptist Church Hymnal, 54
Bengel, 24, 64
Bett, Dr Henry, 9, 10, 30
Bickersteth, Bishop, E. H., 31
Boozers, Converted, 10-12
Bray, Mr, 32
Brevint, Dean, 42-7
Butler, Bishop, 48

CHESTERTON, G. K., 79
Cullman, Oscar, 22

DODD, C. H., 12
Dryden, 53, 55

FABER, 16-18
Fletcher, John, 42, 69

HEIDELBERG CONFESSION, 36
Hügel, the Baron von, 73

JACKSON, DR THOMAS, 32, 36

KINGSWOOD COLLIERS, HYMN WRITTEN FOR, 32-7

LIDGETT, JOHN SCOTT, 48, 49
Lilley, A. L., 73
Luther, 75

MALEFACTORS, 12, 13, 32, 69
Maltby, W. Russell, 63,
Manning, Bernard, 9, 10, 14, 15, 16, 24, 25, 61, 68

Martineau, James, 48
Metaphors of union, 71
Milton, 67
Montefiore, C. G., 76
Moore, Henry, 67-8

NEWGATE PRISON, CHARLES WESLEY AT, 12, 13

OSBORN, DR GEORGE, 19; and see all refs. to *P.W.*
Outcasts, 35-6, 69

PEAKE, A. S., 64
Peterson, Gorlac, 71
Portland, hymn written at, 33, 37-41, 42

RATTENBURY, DR J. ERNEST, 10, 41, 42, 44, 66, 70, 71
Revisions of his work by C. Wesley, 66-7
Robinson, J. Armitage, 24
Ruysbroeck, 71

SMYTH, CANON CHARLES, 10
Spanish Hymn (tr. J. Wesley), 31

TELFORD, JOHN, 9, 33

Veni Creator Spiritus, 20

WATTS, ISAAC, 15, 33, 60, 61
Webb, C. C. J., 71
Wesley, Charles, *passim*
Wesley, John, 13, 15, 21, 25, 26-31, 42, 48, 53, 54, 60, 67

www.ingramcontent.com/pod-product-compliance
Lightning Source LLC
Chambersburg PA
CBHW070059100426
42743CB00012B/2601